THEATRICAL FIGURES
IN PORCELAIN
GERMAN 18TH CENTURY

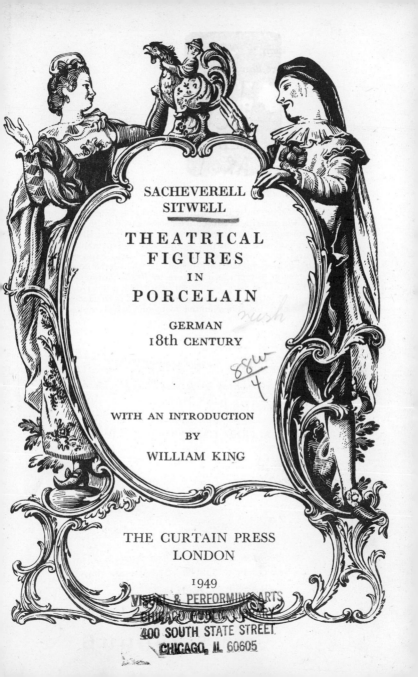

SACHEVERELL
SITWELL

THEATRICAL
FIGURES
IN
PORCELAIN

GERMAN
18th CENTURY

WITH AN INTRODUCTION

BY

WILLIAM KING

THE CURTAIN PRESS
LONDON

1949

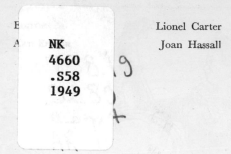
Lionel Carter

Joan Hassall

Acknowledgments

The author and editor wish to thank the Director of the
Victoria and Albert Museum for so courteously giving them
permission and facilities to reproduce the figure illustrated
in colour, and for further permission to reproduce three
figures in monochrome. They wish also to express their
indebtedness to the Director of the British Museum for
permission to reproduce a figure by Franz Anton Bustelli,
and to the Hon. Mrs. Ionides for her great kindness in allow-
ing them to reproduce the several and superb Harlequins
by Johann Joachim Kändler from her private collection.

cover design and decorations by
JOAN HASSALL

colour photography by
ALFRED CARLEBACH, F.R.P.S.

Made and Printed in Great Britain by
STAPLES PRESS LIMITED, ST. ALBANS, HERTS

Blocks by
TESSA PROCESS CO. LTD.

INTRO-
DUCTION

IT is my agreeable task to contribute an introduction to this book which is written by an old friend of mine. This is the first of Sacheverell Sitwell's writings to deal specifically with the art of the potter and it is also the first work to treat of German theatrical porcelain figures.

Porcelain figures as a whole are among the most enchanting manifestations of eighteenth-century miniature sculpture, and the German examples are not the least beautiful. Most of the factories that flourished in that country during the eighteenth century gave birth to theatrical figures of one sort or another. The earliest manufacture was that established at Meissen, near Dresden, and here the presiding genius was Johann Joachim Kändler, who worked in the factory from 1731 until his death in 1775 at the age of sixty-nine. Many of his pupils produced work of decided merit, as did the distinguished modellers of porcelain *Kleinplastik* produced in the other factories that sprang up in different parts of the Empire, starting with Vienna, but it would be tedious to set down a long list of names and dates. Space must be found, however, for the mention of Franz Anton Bustelli, who worked at the factory of Nymphenburg, near Munich, from 1754 to 1763. It is curious that a native of Switzerland, a country not usually associated with masterpieces in the Rococo style, should have been such a master of curve and line.

It only remains to be said that the figures here reproduced are not theatrical in the sense that they portray scenes from the contemporary stage. They are mostly derived from the Italian *Commedia dell' Arte*, which, incidentally, contributed to this country the figures of Harlequin, Columbine and Pantaloon, who graced the harlequinades that now, alas, no longer follow, as of right, the annual Christmas pantomime. Let us hope that this book will incidentally help to reinstate them in the favour of future generations. And now I leave my friend to take up his well-practised pen.

WILLIAM KING.

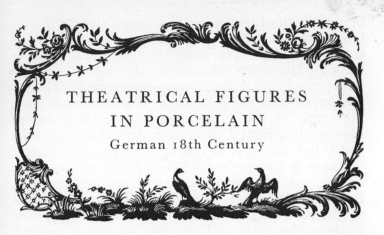

THEATRICAL FIGURES
IN PORCELAIN
German 18th Century

It is one of the tragedies of life, compared to death, that the art of a musician or of an actor perishes with him. When the film is made that is a work of art – when that happens, and not before – this truth may be altered, or be contradicted, but, up till now, nothing is left of musician or stage artist but a cracked record or old photograph. Little, little indeed, do these tell us of what we would like to know. We hear the voice of Caruso, with the magic of Italy, of the Parthenopean gulf and the bay of islands, but fading, fading, it is a voice from another room, from another and dead world; Paderewski, in little pieces by Chopin, or from the *Fantaisiestücke* of Schumann, still strikes the note of poetry and gives us, perhaps, the hundredth part of what he must have been, enough, though, to make us sit still in wonder; while Nijinski in the photographs is a static being, the grasshopper, the cicada upon the ground, not leaping (we call him that because of the huge muscles in his legs and thighs). Gone is the elevation of that prodigious being who had the power to ascend, stay in the air for a moment, and come down slower at what speed he willed. We cannot see him in his leap through the open window as the Spectre of the Rose; nor in his furious, wasp-like beatings against the paper walls in *Petrouchka*. There is something, the ghost of this great dancer, left to us in his photographs from *L'Après-midi*. And that is all, the rest is but memory, or hearsay.

There is this to be said for an old gramophone record, that if you break it, you can buy another. But there exists a category of works of art, exquisite in themselves, but which are irreplaceable, and made to be broken. There are moments, indeed, so fragile are they, when we may wonder how any of them have survived at all. They are porcelain figures; and if, for present purposes, the choice is still further confined so as to include only porcelain figures of actors and dancers then we have arrived at a category of works of art than which nothing could be more evanescent or more fragile. They are, in fact, figures of dancers, principally, though, in order to present them in the fullest detail and in their proper setting, advantage has been taken of the opportunity to surround them with other inhabitants and ornaments of their little world of make believe. In this way something like a complete picture, in miniature, of this chapter in the history of ceramics, or this theatrical sideline, is herewith attempted, and, we will hope, attained.

But, before the curtain rises, certain limitations of material and of technique have to be considered. And we will pose the first question of all; are any of these porcelain figures actual portraits? The question answers itself. One look at our illustrations will show that the porcelain figures are works of fantasy and poetry, only approximating, and perhaps sometimes more by accident than on purpose, to the truth. There can be a portrait in a poem, and a portrait in a piece of music, the practitioner of these arts would tell us, but it may be difficult to recognize the person. There are portraits, certainly, in the early piano pieces of Schumann; and, who could doubt it, in the songs of Schubert? What are Chiarina and Estrella, in *Carnaval*, but sublimated portraits? Even if they be portraits of the same person? The *Novelletten* of Schumann, what are they but groups, or human situations? And we begin to perceive a portrait in a porcelain figure. But these must not be taken entirely, and literally, as portraits. They are reminiscences of person – perhaps more of personality than of physical appearance, when they are portraits at all, which is not often.

Now it has to be established that the art, in general, is one of the arts of the German Rococo. This is one of the lesser, and last delights, of the Italian Renaissance in Europe, and while it may be German in execution, the motif, the subject-matter, more often than not, is Italian. So is it with these porcelain figures of actors and of dancers. The style is Teutonic, but the theme Italian. There were troupes of Italian dancers at many of the small courts of Germany, but, chiefly, at Munich at the court of the Elector of Bavaria, and at Stuttgart, in Wurtemberg. Curiously enough there is less evidence of Italian dancers at the court of Dresden; but entertainments and carousals there were upon such a luxurious scale that it is certain they were present. At Stuttgart there was a large

9

and permanent company of Italian dancers. It is necessary to state these facts in order to set the dancers apart from the Italian comedians, for there is a tendency for many of the porcelain figures to be copied, slavishly, from engravings of the *Commedia dell' Arte*, and whenever this is so, the figures are in decline as works of art. They are never so good when they are under the influence of Callot, or of Watteau. They even cease to be interesting at all, and we have omitted such from our illustrations.

It is, as we say, a Teutonic art, and it has to be considered in relation to others of the minor arts. The Germans, we do not have to remind ourselves, were the greatest of toy makers. Nuremberg was the city in all Europe famous for its toys. What was Doctor Coppelius, in the toy ballet, but a German? It was a sub-Alpine art in its origins, beginning, we may suppose, with the shepherd or herdsmen woodcarving in the long winter evenings when he was shut in by snow. First of all, we are to imagine, he carved wooden animals; and after that, the next step would be wooden toys, figures of human beings that were articulated, that could move their heads and limbs. It was the art, too, of the Christmas tree, with spangles of tinsel or silver paper for the snow upon the pine boughs. Closely connected with this was the art of clock-making, which for some peculiar reason was centred in the mountain valleys. All of these little crafts, in combination, are to be seen in some of the Bavarian mountain churches, Wies, Diessen, or Rottenbuch, which are to be counted among the most delightful specimens of Rococo fantasy in decoration. Churches by the brothers Cosmas Damian and Egid Quirin Asam are the complete parallel or counterpart to the porcelain figures of actors and dancers that we are studying. And, as we shall discover, there is reason to suppose that Ignaz Günther, one of the foremost of the Bavarian wood sculptors, had direct personal influence upon the figures from the Nymphenburg porcelain factory.

In Saxony, the antecedents, perhaps we had better say the ancestors, of the Meissen figures were slightly different in origin, being derived from the sugar or wax figures that were used for ornament upon the banquet tables in the Zwinger. Those readers who have seen this fantastic, fairground palace, one of the most bizarre creations of the Rococo, will be able to carry in their memories the appropriate setting for these banquets. The Zwinger was as impermanent of appearance as the Pavilion at Brighton, and to its fantasy must be added the curious treasures of the Green Vaults, the Grünes Gewölbe, consisting of the goldsmith's work of Dinglinger, and other pantomime treasures of the Saxon Royal collection. . . .

But our attention is caught, suddenly and violently, by the figure of a Harlequin (Plate I). He is sitting upon a whitened tree stump, such a rustic seat as might be imagined in a beer garden, but, also, it is a pedestal for a tropical bird, for some 'papagei', and of course, nothing of the sort, but only the convention of the modeller or sculptor. There have to be stumps or perches where a great many, if not the majority, of the porcelain figures are concerned, and we had better forget about it, for it would be no more reasonable to expect the ballerina to be raised up in the air without the help of her partner. All sculptures, and the little figures in china in particular, have to be given these supports or struts, which, again, are no more to be ignored, and no less to be admired, than the flying buttresses of some Gothic building.

This Harlequin, then, sits on his stump, or pedestal, mug of beer in hand. He takes off his blue hat and waves it with his other hand. It is a curious gesture, and we look at him carefully, for it appears as though he is going to play some trick, pour the beer out of his tankard into his hat, and dash that into someone's face, perhaps, or 'similar', as used to be printed in Mr. B. Pollock's catalogue of pantomime tricks in his Juvenile and Theatrical Tinsel Warehouse, down in Hoxton. But it is a libel upon the Harlequin. He is but taking off his hat and looking slyly, shyly, behind him through the slit eyes in his mask. There is no more in it than that. Yet, all the same, he has that furtive look. He is like some kind of a sly, furtive animal.

He looks back over his shoulder, and we are wondering whom he sees. His mask is black and white, and some 'spots' on his forehead from the firing when he was in the kiln, make him a little bit frightening and forbidding. But, also, take one more look at him, and you will see that because of his mask he is in double profile, that the dark half of his profile looks like a negro face in profile, looks like one of the heads in simultaneous vision, all ways at once, in one of the semi-abstract paintings by Picasso. It is, quite distinctly, a black man, a 'Man Friday', a Caliban, an Othello, whom we see looking out of the Harlequin's face, with his left eye showing. And he becomes, in image, like the soul, the secret in the Harlequin. His cheeks or lozenges are in the brightest colours imaginable; and we admire his belt (one of the only indications of date for it is a relic of the long-waisted surcoats of Le Roi Soleil), his buttons, and his yellow dancing shoes with coloured bows. And there is one more thing to notice. At the back of his mask we can see his yellow, flaxen hair.

He is one of the most engaging of Kändler's Harlequins. This genius of little prodigal inventions (the very name of whom was forgotten at the time, halfway between his own and our's, when the Saxon Schumann was composing Harlequin, Eusebius, Florestan for his *Carnaval*) has left many other Harlequins to choose from – more than there are in all Picasso's paintings put together, more than there were in all the Hoxton dramas. The flaxen hair that we called attention to, a moment ago, suggests that there may have been troupes of travelling players going round to the fairs, and a population of itinerant Saxon actors. For one thing is certain. None of Kändler's Harlequins are Italians.

As if to make the situation more contradictory, and more in character with Harlequin, there exist various versions of this figure with subtle differences in colouring.* In another example belonging to the Hon. Mrs. Ionides, his hat is white, his shoes are black, and his checkers are black and yellow and rose-diamond (indeed they have the exact colouring of a rose-diamond). We illustrate this figure from more than one angle in order to show him in the round (Plate II).

The astonishing ingenuity and grace of this modeller are a delight to follow. For instance, the Harlequin of our opening is a Harlequin indeed. He could be mistaken for no one else. And the same indisputable Harlequin appeared, many and many a time, in the factory at Meissen. It is pleasant to think of the streets of that little town as haunted by him. Unless I am mistaken, there is a painting of Meissen by Bellotto (Canaletto's nephew), a little country town a few miles from Dresden; but, of course, Kändler got his ideas from the cosmopolitan world of the Saxon capital, and I am wondering whether at the fair at Dresden there was not a phenomenon resembling the *balagani* of St. Petersburg, the booths of strolling players who are made immortal in *Petrouchka*.

---

* The figure in the Victoria and Albert Museum has yellow shoes, as described, with red heels and red rosettes; his coat, with gold buttons, has red and yellow checks in front, but they are red and green at the back; one sleeve in blue and white lozenges, the other, black and white; his hat is blue with a gold edge and green rosette, his belt is lilac; his trousers, yellow, turquoise blue and heliotrope.

There is an enchanting, poetical account of them
in Benois' memoirs. After all there was the same
thing at St. Bartholomew's Fair in London. Did
not Kean serve his apprenticeship in Richardson's
show as Harlequin? And Perrot? And Deburau?
The same. They were both Harlequins at fairs.
But the Italian stage episodes in the fairs took on
the local character. We can see it again in Cornelis
Troost's Dutch stage paintings. I believe the only
thing of the kind, still existing, is in the Tivoli
gardens at Copenhagen, where they have an
'Italian' company which has played there since
the eighteenth century. The hero is always Harlequin, and the heroine, Columbine, dressed in the
white *tutu* of a ballerina. The argument is that the
strolling players at Dresden were Saxon, by now;
even if their fathers, or grandfathers, had been
Italian. And this would explain something of the
diversity of Kändler's Harlequins.

For the others of his creation crowd in upon us,
in dumbshow, or uttering their shrill cries. Here is

one in a dancing position (Plate III), masked, smiling, and holding up a huge pair of goggles or spectacles to hide his eyes. And he wears a ruff. He is not so much a crouching animal, a furtive creature, as the other. He has kneebreeches, in lozenges, and white stockings. He has elaborate knots of coloured ribbons on his shoes. But what makes this Harlequin fascinating is that the pattern on his yellow coat is made from playing cards. He is the first of the playing card Harlequins of Kändler, and so far as I know the only evidence for their existence is in Kändler's figures.

He exercised an immense subtlety in them. I have seen Harlequins by Kändler in white suits, with but a single card, perhaps the ace of spades, as passport for their tricks. Or there could be, as well, the different angles and dispositions of the playing cards. A dancing Harlequin (Plate IVa), for instance, given here, with a whole half-dozen – a 'trick' of playing cards – upon the one side of his jacket. And none at all upon the other; and one striped trouser leg; one striped, one plain. And there is the more ordinary, crouching Harlequin (Plate V), but made sinister and menacing with a white mask, like a floured face, and stooping, crouching, his hands low down in front of him. In this instance the mask is a dead end. It does not lend itself, like the mask worn by the first of our Harlequins, to a double or a treble meaning. It means little or nothing. It is expressionless. But what meaning it may have is anything but pleasant. It is the mask of a valet Harlequin out of one of the comedies of Marivaux, making incessant entrances and exits. He has wide diamonds or lozenges of cerise and yellow upon his coat, and gay striped trousers, and appears to be running with some clandestine message.* He is always crouching and quick-moving, a messenger Harlequin or Mercury. But Kändler's Harlequins are endless of invention, and among his most poetical flights of fancy is Harlequin holding a goat (Plate IVb), a pastoral or shepherd Harlequin of peculiar kind for he wears the mask of Mezzetin, thick black whiskers and moustaches upon his floured mask, recalling a remark that has been made before, according to which the origin of Mezzetin may be sought in the unshaved faces of tramps and vagabonds. There are 'sleepers out' to be met with, now, upon the London streets, out of that dwindling population, only a few dozen in number, whom no cajoleries of the Metropolitan Police can induce to sleep indoors, who closely resemble Mezzetin in their bearded masks and suits of patches. One such, well known to me by sight, I met in Piccadilly yesterday. The 'original tramp-cyclist' Jackson, perhaps remembered by some few readers, was his prototype. Now Kändler's Harlequin, whom we are discussing, wears that mask exactly, but he has a curious, high conical hat, which, if only it was black, not white, we could call the Calabrian brigand's hat of Fra Diavolo. He has the long coat of the early eighteenth century, reaching to some way below where our coats reach, but it is a coat of checks or patches, and he has kneebreeches, one leg in patches, one in stripes and zigzags. He sits on the conventional tree stump, carrying the goat upon his knee, and we would call particular

---

* The figure illustrated from the collection of the Hon. Mrs. Ionides has plain, and not striped trousers. There are approximately one hundred figures from the *Commedia dell' Arte* by Kändler, of which the Hon. Mrs. Ionides has all but one in her possession.

attention to his beautiful and sensitive hands, nor omit to notice his guitar; what endless adventure and poetry can be imagined for him! He is one of a new race of Harlequins. A painter whom I know has told me of her delight in drawing in her sketch-book the mere details of the shoes of Kändler's Harlequins, and this pastoral Harlequin is no exception. His legs and feet are advancing, dancing, and we are left to think for ourselves of the comedies in which he played.

And here is Pulcinella (Plate IVc); but much changed from the Pulcinella of the slums of Naples. He wears a close, tight-fitting coat of fish scale pattern, while his far arm and sleeve, could we but see them more distinctly, appear to be in checks or patches. Not only that, but the whole right side of his body, also, so that he is half-Harlequin, half-Pulcinella. And his high peaked hat, except that it has a wide brim, turned up in front, is the hat of the shepherd Harlequin. The theatre is present in his belt and dancing shoes. And in his white trousers, which remind me – how could they do otherwise? – of the white trousers of the pierrots upon the sands, my *balagani*, while I was a child at Scarborough. The pierrots, there, upon the hustings, when the tide was out, and at Catlin's Arcadia upon the Foreshore, were my introduction to the theatre. But one of the most beautiful of Kändler's figures of Harlequins we leave till now; it is Cupid or a little boy as Harlequin (Plate VI), wearing the miniature of the peaked hat we have admired before. He is a little boy about $2\frac{1}{2}$ years old, just able to stand, with his legs bare, but wearing the coat and ruff of Harlequin, and a white mask. This little figure, whether it be by Kändler or not, for the attribution is not certain (it could be by Reinicke), is the perfection of modelling and colouring, but, of course, in strictness it is not a theatrical figure, only an ordinary little boy, and not even an infant member of the Lupino family.

Scaramouche and Columbine of the Italian Comedy – and written thus, we are given the illusion that it still plays, weekly, nightly, like the *Comédie-Française* – are flowered under, not with bouquets, but stray blossoms. The tree stump has become, no rustic bench or perch, but a dead stump with flowers trained upon it in the tradition of the cottage garden in a pantomime or fairy story, while the piece of ground at their feet – shall we say it is no bigger than the area covered by the spotlight? – is strewn with flowers. Scaramouche has the long black cap, almost like a stocking cap, in which we see him in Claude Gillot's paintings. As to that, his figure, more than others that we have described, seems to be influenced by engravings of the Italian Comedy. We admire the large rosettes or buttons on his white jacket, and the black line bordering his ruff, and, as well, the turned-back cuff upon his sleeve. His breeches are black in the photograph, but probably dark blue or plum colour in the original, and this time he has black dancing shoes with buckles. He is making love to Columbine, holding her face and kissing her. She leans her head upon his shoulder and is carrying a birdcage, which she balances upon her hip. She has a dark bodice and a pretty ornament upon her wrist. Neither Scaramouche nor Columbine are dancing. But this pair of creatures are as natural as birds, and have something birdlike in their movements, or he would not be dressed like that, and she

would not be carrying a birdcage. They have come together, we are to imagine, in the middle of an errand.*

Beltrame and Columbine, as a group, are more graceful. Her wide, hooped skirt puts Columbine into the category of one of Kändler's 'crinoline' groups; but we have only to look at photographs of those to know that her's is a stage version; it is not the true aristocratic crinoline. It is Columbine dressed as – what shall we say? – a margravine – this is the suggestion of her hat and ribbons and her corsage which, somehow, is not quite the bodice or corsage of a lady of fashion, while Beltrame wears an antique court suit adapted to the stage. His clothes, be it noted, are not unlike those of the pages in *The Sleeping Beauty*. And what are they doing, we wonder? Is Beltrame leading her before the footlights? (*Vide* cover design.)

But it is not the end of Kändler, even yet. Here is his Turk (Plate XII), a splendid Renaissance Turk out of Venetian paintings. He is earliest seen in Carpaccio, in the paintings at San Giorgio degli Schiavoni and in the picture in the Louvre of the *Stoning of St. Stephen* which, according to some authorities, has medieval Cairo for background. No one, so far as I know, has yet studied the Oriental costumes in these paintings. The same Turkish merchants of Stamboul or Great Cairo appear in Gentile Bellini, but it was Carpaccio, the

---

* Scaramouche and Columbine, taken apart and drawn separately, have been used by Miss Joan Hassall as motif for her title page.

20

Dalmatian, to whom they had particular appeal, and after his time they are dormant in works of art, though present in Venice itself, taking the air in the Piazza and upon the quay, until two hundred and more years later when Tiepolo gave new life to them. There are Turks, the brothers of this Turk of Kändler, in both scenes (we use the theatrical term on purpose) of the *History of Anthony and Cleopatra* in the Palazzo Labia. There are Turkish attendants as they land from the gilded barge and the same Orientals are looking on when Cleopatra dissolves the pearl in wine. In fact the Turkish merchants in their brocaded dresses were a Venetian set piece and we can even see a hint of Turks and Dalmatians in the figures in Canaletto's paintings. This Turk of Kändler is a pantomime character, and as such, included here; but he is not much exaggerated and until the reign of Mahmoud the Reformer (d. 1839) this was the Turkish costume. These Turks were merchants or sea captains. Personal wealth in Turkey was expressed upon the person, and these glorious pantomime characters had little or no furniture or other belongings in their homes. The tradition of the Turks will have reached Kändler through any traveller, for it could almost be said that sumptuous costume was the art of the Ottomans, heirs and conquerors of Byzantium. This is the explanation of the beautiful and incredible dress of a little town like Scutari, near Ragusa, and of the dresses of the Albanians and of the Greek islands. The white cloak of Kändler's Turk has its prototype in the white cloaks of Carpaccio in his *Stoning of St. Stephen*. But, also, there are many other figures of Turks by Kändler; Turks playing lutes or guitars, and seated Turks, crosslegged, with sweetmeat dishes upon their knees, certain figures, too, of Turkish janissaries with the high, folded caps upon their heads.

Kändler modelled figures of Poles, as well, in their semi-Oriental dress – no feat of imagination, for Dresden and Warsaw during much of his lifetime were the two capitals of the Electors of Saxony, who, despite their Lutheran background, had turned Catholic in order to become eligible for the throne of Poland. There were many Poles in the streets of Dresden. The Poles, as I have seen for myself in portraits in old Polish country houses, were probably the only nation in Europe who preserved national dress among the upper classes and did not surrender to the universal periwig – instead, they shaved their heads and wore long moustachios, high boots, and caftans. Polish ladies wore the ordinary fashions of the day, and it is for this reason that a well known group by Kändler of a Polish gentleman kissing a lady's hand presents this contrast in the dresses of the man and woman.

Kändler is most famous for his 'crinoline' groups which in spite of their exaggerated artificiality can hardly be included here as groups of actors or of dancers. This is a pity because many of them are little masterpieces of graceful invention. His poetical sense seized upon the hooped skirt as being one of the most suitable of mediums to be portrayed in china. A separate publication could, of course, be devoted to these 'crinoline' groups and they should be drawn and photographed from every angle. They are one of the extreme artificialities of all the ages. But there was hardly any form of modelling in porcelain to which Kändler did not

BLACKAMOOR LEADING A SPANISH HORSE.
Meissen; by J. J. Kändler.

turn his hand; and this, waiving the theatrical limits of the present occasion, must be our opportunity to mention his white horses led by blackamoors, his birds (jays, storks, hoopoes, cockatoos), dogs (little red and white Bologna terriers, and pugs, lately imported from China for the first time), goats and other animals. His profuse and prodigal talents found an outlet in the 'Swan Service', made for Count Brühl, all of which, in every detail, is a poetical allegory upon the theme of water. The great tureens of this service have swans modelled upon them, and there are swans on every dish, down to the little salt cellars. I am not the first writer to mention the name of the great Bernini, when thinking of the 'Swan Service'. For it does seem as prodigal of invention as Bernini if we consider his Roman fountains as another poetical allegory upon water, and here the invention is of the same order of originality. This 'Swan Service' would be a sensation in itself were there no other works extant from the hand of Kändler.*

One has no sooner got to admire, in particular, some phase in Kändler's porcelain figures than one is carried off in rapture by another. That he was fully conscious of the ease of his own talents is evident in one of his memoranda addressed to the directors of the Meissen manufactory in which he discusses the design of handles for cups and coffee pots and comments upon the endless and infinite variety that it was possible to give to them. No detail was too little for his attention. But it will be found, his birds and animals apart, and except for his 'crinoline' groups and for the 'Swan Service'

---

* The 'Swan Service' is, or was, in possession of Count Brühl's descendants at Schloss Pförten in Upper Lusatia. Where is it now?

that his figures taken from the theatre are the most beautiful of his creations. The Venetian 'Avvocato' (Plate XIII), it is true, takes on an added poetical or literary interest as soon as it is known that he, too, is of the theatre. For, at first sight, he is a Venetian citizen from one of Longhi's little paintings. How fragile and poetically beautiful are the long trailing sleeves of the 'Avvocato'! A beautiful passage in the texture and substance of porcelain! For he is the lawyer of the Venetian comedy, in the long gown of the lawyer, and carrying a roll of papers in his hand. And he wears the *bauta*, the mask of the Carnival of Venice. This was the most wonderful of European spectacles, beside which even the Feria of Seville is but little, and the 'Avvocato', stage figure though he be, is an understatement compared to many of the pedestrian characters that could be seen (we call them 'pedestrian', because, in other cities, they would be driving in coaches, riding on horseback, or carried in sedan chairs, but, here, in Venice, they were on foot, always), in the Piazza, or stepping from the gondola. The 'Avvocato' is unexaggerated, compared to many of them, while, perhaps, the most that could be said against him as a work of art is that he is too unexceptional and typical, too much the porcelain figure, and too little the actor, or, in fact, the 'Avvocato'. Perhaps, too, the texture is more glass than porcelain; and I have seen figures from the modern glass works in Murano which, technically, stand at no long distance from the 'Avvocato'.

But Kändler can be forgotten and there are, still, the other wares of Meissen. So fanciful are the early arabesque figures painted in black and red and gold, in silhouette, by Herold, upon chocolate and coffee services that they could be characterized as theatre subjects. They are derived from Callot in style and manner, through such entire works of the imagination as the engravings from the Dutchman Romeyn de Hooge's *Les Indes Orientales et Occidentales*. This, again, is in Callot's manner and influenced, as well, by Stefano della Bella. Tea, coffee, chocolate, were still substances of romance and mystery in the early eighteenth century, in association with the figures seen in tapestries of *Les Indes Galantes*, and so forth, and upon lacquer cabinets. It is Confucian China, really a pictorial invention of the European; and deriving, too, from the figures on Dutch atlases and portolan charts. This was at a time when much of the Meissen porcelain was copied directly from Japanese porcelain, a phase, too, which was undergone by Chelsea and by Worcester. No one then knew the difference, aesthetically, between India (and there are three Indies – Hindu, Moslem, East Indian) and China, or Japan. And in the result, the silhouette figures of Herold, which are typical of much of the poetical confusion in tapestries and upon pieces of lacquer, if they are the pictorial truth of any civilization there has ever been, look Korean. It is of the white garments and black lacquer hats of Korea that they remind us, where Confucian beards are still worn by the aged literati, and the costume is, in fact, the Ming dress, preserved, of ancient China. The 'Kakiemon' pieces of Meissen, literal copies or adaptations from the Japanese, have a charm of their own, and there are, of course, a large number of figures of Chinamen by Kändler, and other modellers. Pertaining to this Confucian China, that we have described as a literary or poetical concept, are the seated mandarins who nod their heads, and lift and let fall their hands. Their precise origin may be in Chinese street toys, or in figures of gods or demons from the crowded temples of Canton, but they soon take on another character and would no longer be worshipped in the joss houses. Kändler was one of the most prolific inventors of these Chinamen who in the degree of their divergence from reality approximate more and more nearly to figures on the stage. Such are the so-called 'Malabars', their very name an indication of geographical ignorance and inexactitude, figures with big heads and wearing gigantic hats. We illustrate an extravagantly conceived and fanciful figure of a Chinaman riding astride upon some barnyard relative of the golden cockerel (Plate XIV). But, also, there are groups of Chinamen, who are nothing more or less than figures from a 'Chinese' ballet. These had a particular influence upon Nicholas Sprimont and the modellers of Chelsea china, and some of them are among the most beautiful of all groups of porcelain. There are young girls with 'Chinese' foreheads but European features, with graceful children playing at their feet; and again there are 'Chinese' children influenced by the dwarves of Callot.

Meissen is the half, or hardly that, of German porcelain. And I suppose the other most famous factory is that of Nymphenburg, a creation of the Bavarian Electors, housed in one wing of the palace of that name, outside Munich, and in close proximity, therefore, to the pavilion of the Amalienburg. This hunting pavilion, one of the wonders of the Rococo, was designed by Cuvilliés, the court dwarf, of French-Walloon descent, who showed talent at an early age and was sent by the Elector to study his art in Paris, under Blondel. He also built the Residenz-Theater, attached to the palace in Munich, and now destroyed, which we mention because it is important to realize the circumstances of artificiality in which the Nymphenburg porcelain was designed and made. One of the great stage designers of the Italian school, Francesco Santuzini, had built a sham *Bucintoro*, in imitation of that of Venice, upon the formal canal and sheet of water in front of the Nymphenburg palace. This pleasure craft, a kind of Armida's galleon, with great painted sails, and rowed by eighty rowers with scarlet oars, was used for theatrical entertainments, by night, with fireworks, and for banquets after the great hunting parties. Conditions were, in fact, propitious for every conceivable form of theatrical entertainment and extravagance, and the porcelain factory at Nymphenburg must have been almost a minor item in the repertoire.

But the Electors had the services of Franz Anton Bustelli, after Kändler the most gifted of all the modellers of porcelain figures. He was, in fact, much more extreme and mannered, and will appeal to some tastes as more interesting and violent in originality. He was an Italian-Swiss, from near Lugano, in the Canton of Tessin (Ticino), and his affinity is to the mountain woodcarvers, of whom he was a sort of monstrous or diseased offspring in the same way that Beardsley is an abnormal and exceptional growth upon Fred Walker, Pinwell, and the woodcut illustrators of the 'sixties. *The Marriage of Figaro* is such another magical growth upon the corpse of comedy with music. The

ISABELLA (?) AND PIERROT (?) WITH LANTERN. *Nymphenburg;* by F. A. Bustelli.

rarefied attitudinous works of the Nymphenburg porcelain factory are of another mood, another generation from those of Meissen. It is the Bavarian Rococo compared with the Handelian Saxon (for Handel, also, was a Saxon), and many tastes that cannot accept the Bavarian fantasy in architecture are ready to welcome it in china. In England, we may like to remember, the taste of our countrymen rejected the Rococo as a whole, and only allowed it upon a few stucco ceilings, in furniture and looking-glasses, and in the porcelain of Worcester and of Chelsea. But, in Bavaria, visual life from the *Schloss* to the châlet was Rococo, more completely, indeed, than in any land in Europe. The Rococo was the vernacular;

and Franz Anton Bustelli passed easily into it, moving from one side of the mountains to the other. His dates correspond closely to those of Egid Quirin and Cosmas Damian Asam, and the stimulation can be imagined of creating, not outside and against the current of contemporary life, but in the midst of it, and lifting yourself, by your own efforts, so often and easily out of the stream. In order to be conspicuous it was only necessary to go a little further, and perhaps the effortless ease of this creation can be argued by recalling the open air exhibition of sculpture, last summer, in Battersea Park. Those ugly and unhappy forms indicate the character of the age we live in, only relieved by the huge metaphors and symbols of a Henry Moore.

Bustelli, as a modeller, worked instinctively towards the theatre. His green huntsmen and ladies in riding habits are worthy of the second act, the hunting scene of *The Sleeping Beauty*. His 'crinoline' groups identify themselves with the characters in *Così fan Tutte*, so that we have in our ears the miraculous orchestral accompaniment interpreting their thoughts and emotions. This is not to say, for it would be ridiculous, that Bustelli's figures are upon a plane with Mozart's invention in his operas for, of course, in comparison they are but little works of art, but the same light or refulgence has been shed upon them, or it could be said in parable, that they are emanations of the same planet. They are more theatrical, by far, than the 'crinoline' groups of Kändler. They are more theatrical, even, in their texture, or in the very materials of the hooped dresses, for they are no longer the brocaded gowns of Kändler, often with patterns of flowers upon them that would be beautiful upon a Meissen dinner service. The dresses of Bustelli, more often than not, are self-coloured; they are selfs, in the sense in which florists and fanciers use that term. They are always conceived visually, not, as with Kändler, to look the more beautiful the more nearly they are examined, but to satisfy the spectator from far off, from his seat on the sofa, in the box, or in the row of stalls; and the nearer you get to them, to the point of touching them and taking them in your hand, the more surprised you are by the cleverness of the illusion. They are not dolls or puppets, but figures intended to be seen as large as life, and which you get to know from a distance. Indeed, the trouble with Bustelli's figures, when it was the question of choosing the illustrations for this number of *The Masque* is that so many of them are theatrical or ballet subjects in all but fact. They are huntsmen, let us say, but despite their suitability and their decided leaning towards the stage it is not possible to include them as actors or as dancers. This is not the case, though, with the newly acquired Leda, in the British Museum (Plate XV). This lady, if correctly named, is an unexpected, but welcome addition to the *Commedia dell'Arte*. She shows Bustelli in every beauty of his modelling with her green crinoline and upraised arm. It is a lovely example of his restraint and grace.

There was a time, not long ago, when Meissen in popular opinion meant German porcelain, and little was known about the other factories. Kändler was, then, the great modeller, but while the extra-ordinary range and diversity of his talent emerge more and more, there is the tendency, now, to regard Franz Anton Bustelli as the genius of the porcelain figure. He is looked upon as more

interesting, aesthetically, than Kändler, in whom
an uniform excellence in conception and execution
tended to produce a dead level, one of those surface
similarities, say, under which so many varying
degrees and depths are hidden, like the eighty
quartets or the hundred or more symphonies of
Haydn. Could it not be said that Bustelli was more
original in theme, and less original in variation?
He did not work out anything like the same number
of Chinamen, ladies in hooped skirts, or whatever
the subject might be, but his variations though
fewer, were each the occasion for closer and more
searching thought. Sometimes he would leave his
figures uncoloured, as though their shape and out-
line were enough, and this is one of the simpler
subtleties that never dawned on Kändler. It is in
this connection that the influence of the woodcarver Ignaz Günther must be sought, for he was
probably associated with the Nymphenburg porcelain factory soon after its foundation. The flat
planes of the woodcarver when he attempts dramatic
effect, without realism of detail, were transferred
by Bustelli into porcelain. It was a new technique
in china modelling and, eventually, he carried it
to further lengths than was possible in the sculptor's
studio. There are groups by Bustelli (one of them
is in the Victoria and Albert Museum) which,
probably, could be carried out in no other material
but potter's clay, or plasticine. They consist of a
rounded or elliptical base, which could be compared to a floating island, and this has been worked
into stage mounds or hillocks with figures standing
at different levels, dogs coming out of tunnels or
warrens, with trees, flowers, any other objects
Bustelli liked and, always, Rococo scrolls and

floreated planes (if that describes them), textures, again, which could only be expressed in wood, or in the lath and canvas of the scene painter. But, even more original is Bustelli's sense of colour. His latent stage sense is apparent in the skill with which he satisfies the spectator and keeps him at a distance. It is, as it were, a concession to the social scene, an acknowledgment that he had to impose himself in the midst of chatter and conversation – a parallel, therefore, to the music that Mozart had to compose that was performed during the Prince-Bishop of Salzburg's dinners, or while people were talking in their boxes at the opera.

To the artist, in any of the arts, there is much pleasure and little profit in Kändler, and an infinity of ideas to be had from Bustelli. Novels and plays could be inspired by him, the reason being that his treatment, more than his achievement, is the rich lode or vein of theory. Bustelli is one of those artists who make their statement and pass on, who have not entirely expressed themselves to the far limits of execution. Kändler, perhaps, is fuller and happier in temperament, but he was of an earlier generation. There is no sign of torment in him. And no experiment; only an endless flow of creation. But Bustelli belonged to the rare order of experimental Rococo; or again, taking our parallels from an earlier and greater period, and using for our purposes some of the greatest and most famous names, where Kändler corresponds (all allowance made for difference of stature and proportion) to Bernini, Bustelli is the Borromini of the porcelain figure. Bustelli is an influence for the future; Kändler is complete in himself. Little or nothing more is to be gleaned from him.

CAVALIER AND LADY IN A HOOPED DRESS. *Nymphenburg;* by F. A. Bustelli.

A 'Lady in a Crinoline' by Bustelli has more
movement than the 'crinoline' groups of Kändler.
She is a figure, not a figurine. Her arms express
that she is walking, moving, and we hear the
rustling of her dress. She has, which is not usual with
Bustelli, a pattern of flowers upon her hooped skirt;
but the modelling of her bodice, of her neck and
shoulders, is more subtle than in Kändler's figurines.
She is a living person, observed; and not a mere
doll or puppet. Bustelli had a flight of his own of
female figures from Italian Comedy whom it is
difficult to identify. He was more interested, it
is evident, in stage figures taken from life than
in ordinary living persons. Their thin shoulders
make it evident they are not opera singers. They
are actors or ballet dancers. The male figures

34

of Bustelli are his weakness; they are affected and attitudinized. His figure of Ottavio Kissing his Hand, in the Victoria and Albert museum, has a note of effeminacy which never occurs in Kändler. His male figures, therefore, are theatrical in the bad sense, in that they are mannered and affected. Nevertheless, Bustelli is the most inspired and original of all the modellers of porcelain figures.

But this fragile and evanescent art had its moments in remote places, and where least expected. If we are looking for actors and dancers we would expect to find them at Ludwigsburg. This model town, and dull echo (architecturally) of Versailles, was built by Duke Eberhard Ludwig* (d. 1733) to the design of the Italian Frisoni. But his porcelain factory, minor but indispensable adjunct to a German princeling, is disappointing for our purpose. Figures of dancers, perhaps the most difficult branch of the whole art of modelling in porcelain, are inferior and few in number. They are 'difficult', of necessity, since at a court with the peculiar amenities of Ludwigsburg the figures could not be pure fantasy. They must bear some likeness to the original. It must be for this reason that Ludwigsburg was more successful in its figures of Chinamen. An Italian, Domenico Ferretti, worked here as modeller; but his Celestials are those of Buen Retiro and Capodimonte, which is to say they are china Chinamen, and little more. The straw hats in three tiers, like a pagoda, are not more Chinese than the straw cloaks and hats of the

---

* The great Noverre was employed by his successor, Duke Karl Eugen, who had three theatres, one French and two Italian. Servandoni designed the scenery, Bocquet the dresses, Jomelli was conductor. There were twenty principal dancers, and one hundred in the *corps-de-ballet*. Casanova gives a sprightly account of this delightful and deleterious temple of the dance.

peasants in Portugal, along the Douro, where the wine is brought down in boats with huge rudders to Oporto, and his children are but ordinary children with a Tartar topknot. In fact, their fantasy is not far fetched enough, and the Ludwigsburg china is better in coffee cups and saucers, and the humbler things. Other factories where the porcelain, on occasion, is of the highest possible quality, Höchst, for example, are equally disappointing, if it be for actors and dancers that we are searching.

But, as so often in the pursuit of works of art, the existence of something which seems hypothetical and to be desired, turns out, in the end, to have been accomplished and to have surpassed itself. It can even have crossed from the region of the ordinary into that of the exceptional and transcendental. The lover of porcelain who discovers for himself the beggars and salt miners of Johann Joachim Kändler, and progresses through his birds or spaniels to his monkey-musicians, 'crinoline' groups, 'pagodas' (squatting figures of Chinamen), 'Malabars', and eventually, to the 'Swan Service' and the glittering array of Harlequins, will, next, look greedily through Bustelli's figures, admiring them for certain qualities of poetry and imagination that are his own, and that are not to be found in the porcelain of Meissen, and yet will not be satisfied. There is still something lacking.

The porcelain figures of Frankenthal, in the Palatinate, provide the answer. They are by the modeller J. W. Lanz, of whom little else is known, and who worked at Frankenthal for a few years only (1755-61). A Pierrot (not illustrated) from his hand is unexceptional, and I would suggest that it may have been a 'fill-up' done in order to complete a series of comedians. The figure is more Mezzetin than Pierrot, in his striped silk coat, and breeches. He has, certainly, the hat of Mezzetin. Yet, something in his attitude is Pierrot more than Mezzetin.

His companions dwell in a world apart; a dancing Pierrot, Harlequin, and Columbine. And of the three it is the first and last-mentioned that are transcendental and of prime order. The Harlequin (Plate XVIc) is a dancing figure; as behold his arm akimbo, his hand that lifts his hat, his legs in white trousers, and his dancing shoes! His Joseph's coat of many colours is gay as any patchwork quilt. But he lifts his hat as though to introduce us to his companions. They stand on their little porcelain rafts or bases which, once again, are prophetic of the spotlight. Pierrot (Plate XVIa) balances upon his, and is moving swiftly. He comes forward with the light upon him. His trousers and the curve of his body prove him to be a dancer; but it is, above all, in the balance of his arms, one higher than the other, and beating upon the air. They are wings or flails that support him, and this is given emphasis in the curious construction of his sleeves, which are of a form I do not remember having seen before in any painting or engraving. It is obvious, I think, that these sleeves are in character with him. His hands have come out of his sleeves, to help him dancing, and at other moments they are hidden, which is when he is the sentimental Pierrot who is too familiar, of whom too much has been seen and written. He has a white ruff or corolla, black mask, and hat of unusual shape. He has no Pierrot buttons.

Columbine (Plate XVIb) is an enchanting blend of Pierrot and Harlequin. In fact, granted their whole companies or regiments, she is dressed like the *vivandière* of either; that is to say, she wears the feminine version of their uniform; white, full skirt, in compliment to the white trousers of Pierrot, Harlequin's jacket, black mask, and Pierrot's white hat. She anticipates the Harlequina of the London pantomimes, who was not to make her appearance for another hundred years. But one glance at her only, and you will know the century to which she belongs, in her length and shape of skirt, not yet shortened into the *tutu*, the ballet skirt, and also, in her jacket, which is the bodice of another age, altogether. Her arms, again, are beautiful in modelling, and she is moving slowly in some dance, gavotte or saraband, something slow and stately, not related, at all, to classical dancing as it is known to-day, which is the invention of Italian and French masters. The Pierrot is a more agile dancer; but in Columbine (or Harlequina) something is missing. And her secret we will keep till last.

Here, too, at the end of this essay, we will discuss the Pierrot of the beginning, in the coloured plate (*vide* frontispiece). He is of the Klosterveilsdorf porcelain factory, a small concern founded by Duke Wilhelm Eugen of Saxe-Hildburghausen, a Thuringian princeling. The modeller seems not to be known; but there is little doubt that this is the most beautiful of all the porcelain figures of actors and dancers. At the moment of writing, the lime-green, daffodil-yellow Pierrot of Klosterveilsdorf seems to be entirely original in conception, and not to be copied from some print in a book of plays, or from an engraving. This could be contradicted at any time by the discovery of his prototype, but it would not alter the beauty of his colour. The whip, like a postillion whip, carried in his right hand, suggests that he is a Pierrot in some incident or predicament out of a play, and this drama could in all probability be identified. But the colouring of Pierrot, even though he be copied exactly in stance and position, is a most beautiful poetical invention. I have never heard before in my life of a yellow Pierrot, less still of a Pierrot who is lime-green, but the colour fits his temperament.

He is not masked. His face is in its natural colours. But he is thinking or pondering, and holds his finger in his mouth. He has had a rebuff of some sort, or is wondering what he will do next. His attitude is entirely in character. He is *Le Grand Gilles* of the Thuringian forests. Watteau's masterpiece in the Louvre was painted in about 1720, and this porcelain figure dates from 1775. How slowly the news travelled! He is two generations later than *Le Grand Gilles*, and will appear again in the person of Deburau and in the poems of Verlaine. What is he doing in the Thuringer-Wald? If, indeed, he ever played in these regions, alike, in his instance and in the Gilles of Watteau's picture, the person playing the part was a young man. It is important to remember this. It is unthinkable that an old, even a middle-aged man, should play the part of Pierrot. Which is no sooner said than contradicted, for Deburau played Pierrot until his death, when he was nearer fifty than forty years old. But Deburau was altogether exceptional, and as we can tell from the early photograph by Nadar (taken in 1846) he must have been one of the most poetical actors who ever lived. Nadar's portrait of him is one of the rare photographs that is a work of art, and I would suggest that this head of Deburau, together with

Joan Hassall

Lous XV and La Pompadour as *Acis* and *Galatea. Meissen;* by J. J. Kändler.

Watteau's immortal *Le Grand Gilles*, and the lime-green porcelain figure of Klosterveildsorf, are the witnesses or evidence for Pierrot.

This brings us to the end of our repertory of old porcelain figures of actors and dancers. There are, in fact, but few of them. The only plentitude is in Kändler's Harlequins. Those are a troupe or company to themselves. There are enough to choose, or to reject, among. But the others are so rare that they have to be taken as they stand. There are and must be many difficulties attending the modelling of actual dancers. To make a figure of an Italian comedian required little more than the mere copying of an engraving. The original was static. It would stand still for as long as needed. But the dancer must be in movement, and must be like the dancer. Of how many of the figures illustrated is this true? Some of them do, certainly, seem to be closely observed. The Harlequins of Kändler must be taken as projections of his fantasy. The dancers and actors of Nymphenburg, due to Bustelli, are no more actors and dancers than most of his other figures. They could all be described indiscriminately as theatrical or of the theatre. The Frankenthal Pierrot and Harlequin are, at once, more beautiful and more accurate than any of the other figures. The Pierrot of Klosterveilsdorf is standing still. He is not dancing. The Frankenthal figures by J. W. Lanz, particularly the Pierrot, are in movement; but it is not dancing as that is known to-day. The first pictures of that are in the lithographs of Taglioni, Elssler, Grisi, and what are in reality, by one of those contradictions so common in the theatre, the classical dancers of the Romantic Ballet – lithographs, most of them, of London origin and dating from the eighteen-forties. In fact, they are a hundred years later than the heyday of the porcelain figure.

There is no such thing, therefore, as an eighteenth-century porcelain figure of a dancer standing upon her points. This was first practised by Taglioni, and it may be looked upon as one of the innumerable lesser tragedies in art that this supreme invention in the art of dancing, or it is in fact the whole art, in principle, of the ballerina, should have appeared after the slow decline and death of porcelain. It is sad, because a figure of a dancer in porcelain has an intrinsic beauty, only as an idea. It is beautiful, already, before it is begun. With regard to the present, and to the future, moreover, it is one of those arts that can be helped, legitimately, by the camera. In the fever, or rage, for ballet in our time it is curious that no modeller has revived the art; not more surprising, though, than that no composer has appeared who can write the proper music. There could be beautiful porcelain figures of the ballerinas of our time. We need only remember Margot Fonteyn or Moira Shearer in the swans-down headdress of *Lac des Cygnes*, or in the black and gold bodice and *tutu* of Odette in Act III; in the rose-pink and silver of Princess Aurora in *The Sleeping Beauty*, and in the yellow *tutu* of the last scene; as Giselle; as Swanilda in *Coppélia*; as the present *Cinderella*, in order to know that this is true. There could be no better theme than the classical ballets, performed now at Covent Garden as nowhere else in the world. The climaxes of the great set dances of Petipa, of the 'Rose' adagio, for an example, in *The Sleeping Beauty*, or, again, Princess Aurora's solo in Act I, and her *pas de deux* and solo in Act III, the Blue Bird (the most famous and applauded *pas* in the whole art of dancing); the waltz of Odette in *Lac des Cygnes*, followed by her variation with the thirty-two *fouettés*, surely these should be inspiration enough for the modeller of china figures!

In evidence of these possibilities there are the beautiful, but little seen, Meissen figures, the existence of which was unknown to me until a few weeks ago, in spite of considerable personal knowledge of the Russian Ballet, and memories extending back over many years. They are modern Meissen figures made just before the 1914 war by Paul Scheurich, a German modeller who revived the art. There are five figures in all from Fokine's *Carnaval*.* All six principal dancers are shown; Nijinski and Karsavina (in the group) Eduardova, Fokina, Novikoff, and Bolm. Karsavina's fluttering skirt is a beautiful passage in porcelain, but Nijinski as Harlequin is in an exaggerated pose, almost reminiscent of Dantan's caricature statuette of Paganini. Here, at last, we see the ballerina on her points! How lightly and beautifully Fokina (as Estrella) moves upon the blocked toes of her ballet shoes! And to think that Fokine and Fokina, when I met them in 1937 or 1938, were no longer young! For Fokina in her billowing skirt has a fragile and immortal youth. Scheurich modelled his figures from photographs and from Bakst's original drawings, which he elaborated slightly, for instance, in the flowers on Eduardova's bodice. But action photography, since that day, has advanced out of nothing into an art which could be of the greatest practical help to the designer; and before it is too late, let us see figures

---

* These figures are illustrated in *Ballet*, for November 1948.

of the ballerina in those great moments that we mentioned, held by her partner, at the climax and flowerhead of the dance.

Look again at the Pierrot of Klosterveilsdorf! He is thinking, waiting for something. There is an immediacy in his movement and his attitude. Or it is something that has just happened, and that leaves him speechless, not knowing what to do or say. Little doubt what it is! The art of the porcelain figure is a little art and it depends upon the shock of fresh surprise. To find the figure as you remember it, yet never quite the same! Such is the secret of the art. And it is, also, one of the secrets of the stage. That is why there is a particular and appropriate beauty in the few actors and dancers now assembled, and who now disperse. So close the page! And when you open it again, like living actors they will have moved or spoken. Ring down the curtain! Leave them in darkness! Or turn on the lights! It is all the same to them. They are dead, but living figures. They live when we look at them; and in this they are luckier than actors, whose art dies with them. They are small and fragile, and one of the minor beauties of the age of reason. This is their one and only performance, and it is playing all the time.

I.   A HARLEQUIN. *Meissen;* by J. J. Kändler.

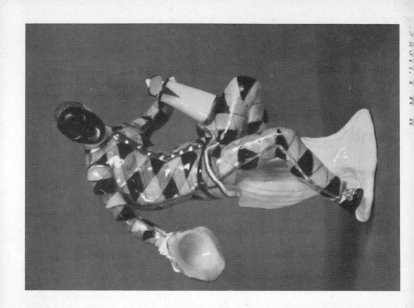

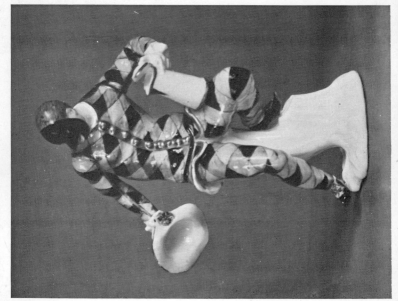

III. A Dancing Harlequin. *Meissen;* by J. J. Kändler.

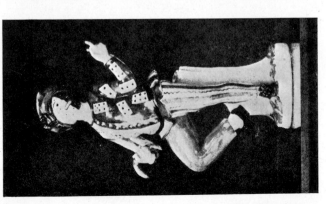

IV. (a) A Dancing Harlequin (b) A Harlequin Holding a Goat (c) Pulcinella. *Meissen;* all by J. J. Kändler.

V.   A Crouching Harlequin. *Meissen;* by J. J. Kändler.

VI. A BOY AS HARLEQUIN. *Meissen;* by J. J. Kändler or Peter Reinicke.

VII.   A HARLEQUIN. *Meissen;* by J. J. Kändler.

VIII.   A Harlequin. *Meissen;* by J. J. Kändler.

IX. A HARLEQUIN. *Meissen;* by J. J. Kändler.

X.   A HARLEQUIN TEASING A DOG. *Meissen;* by J. J. Kändler.

XI. A HARLEQUIN TEASING A MONKEY. *Meissen;* by J. J. Kändler.

XII. A TURK. *Meissen;* by J. J. Kändler.

XIII. AN AVVOCATO. *Meissen;* by J. J. Kändler.

XIV.　A Chinese Astride a Cockerel. *Meissen;* by J. J. Kändler.

XV. Leda (?) *Nymphenburg;* by F. A. Bustelli.

XVI. (a) PIERROT (b) COLUMBINE (c) A DANCING HARLEQUIN. *Frankenthal*; all by J. W. Lanz.